The Unregulated Dark

The Unregulated Dark

Dakota Frandsen

LEGAL DISCLAIMER AND LIMITATION OF LIABILITY

The information contained in this book—including but not limited to sample letters, checklists, legislative proposals, and legal templates—is provided for informational purposes only. The author and publisher have made every effort to ensure the accuracy of the information within this book was correct at time of publication. The author and publisher do not assume and hereby disclaim any liability to any party for any loss, damage, or disruption caused by errors or omissions, whether such errors or omissions result from negligence, accident, or any other cause.

This document is for educational and drafting purposes only. It does not constitute legal advice. Consult a qualified attorney in your jurisdiction for specific legal actions.

The author and publisher are not attorneys, and the content within does not create an attorney-client relationship. Laws regarding property rights, defamation, privacy, trespassing, and criminal statutes vary significantly by state, province, and country. The templates and strategies outlined herein should not be used as a substitute for professional legal counsel, nor should they be used to confront dangerous individuals without law enforcement assistance.

CONTENTS

INTRODUCTION: The Unregulated Dark

Why We Need a Legal Shield Against the Supernatural Industry

If you walk into a private investigator's office, you will see a license on the wall. That license guarantees that the person behind the desk has passed a background check, carries liability insurance, and operates within the bounds of the law. If they harass you, stalk you, or break into your home, they lose their livelihood and face immediate prosecution.

Now, imagine a different kind of investigator. One who enters the homes of grieving families, claiming to speak with their dead children. One who breaks into abandoned hospitals and private residences under the cover of night, armed with cameras and crowbars. One who carries a weapon for "spiritual protection" and answers to no licensing board, no oversight committee, and no code of ethics.

This is the modern "Paranormal Investigator."

For decades, society has viewed ghost hunting, cryptozoology, and demonology as harmless eccentricities—a fringe hobby for thrill-seekers and folklore enthusiasts. But in the age of social media, the algorithmic monetization of fear has transformed this quirk into a dangerous, unregulated industry. The "haunted" sector is no longer about flashlights in a graveyard; it is about content, clout, and cash. And in the rush to capture the next viral "evidence," the line between curiosity and criminality has been obliterated.

The Predator's Camouflage

The primary purpose of this book is to strip away the romanticized veneer of the "ghost hunter" and reveal the stark legal reality underneath. We are not here to debate the existence of ghosts, Bigfoot, or demons. We are here to address the very real, very human predators who use these concepts as a shield for criminal behavior.

The "supernatural community" currently operates as a perfect camouflage for predation. Because the field requires no credentials, anyone can declare themselves an expert "Demonologist" or "Intuitive Medium."

- **Sexual Predators** use this self-appointed authority to groom vulnerable women and children, claiming they need to perform "cleansings" or "energy work" that crosses physical boundaries.
- **Con Artists** exploit the bereaved, selling them communication with deceased loved ones using devices that are nothing more than random word generators.
- **Vigilantes** weaponize their followers, launching digital harassment campaigns against skeptics or private homeowners who refuse to grant them access to "haunted" properties.

The True Crime Crossover

Perhaps most concerning is the recent collision between the paranormal community and active police investigations. We have entered an era of "True Crime Tourism," where amateur sleuths and psychics descend upon the scenes of fresh tragedies. They trample crime scenes, contaminate evidence, distract law enforcement with "visions," and harass the families of victims—all under the guise of "helping the spirits find justice." This is not investigation; it is obstruction of justice, and it is actively hindering the resolution of real-world crimes.

The Vacuum of Accountability

Why does this continue unchecked? Because our legal system has not caught up. When a homeowner calls the police to report a group of ghost hunters trespassing, officers often treat it as a nuisance call rather than a break-in. When a victim reports they are being "cursed" or stalked by a coven, authorities may dismiss it as a civil dispute between eccentrics.

Law enforcement lacks the framework to see these actions for what they are: **Stalking. Fraud. Trespassing. Child Abuse.**

How to Use This Book

This book is a weapon of self-defense. It is designed to bridge the gap between the "spooky" and the "statutory."

- **For the Property Owner:** You will find the legal language necessary to bar these groups from your land and protect your property's value from being "stigmatized" by viral rumors.
- **For the Victim:** You will find the checklists needed to translate your harassment into admissible evidence for a police report.
- **For Law Enforcement:** You will find the precedents and statutes that reclassify "paranormal activity" into prosecutable offenses (seek legal counsel applicable to your jurisdiction).

The shadows may be unregulated, but the people hiding in them are not. It is time to turn on the lights.

Analysis Report

1. Executive Summary

The burgeoning, yet fundamentally unregulated, field of paranormal investigation—a broad umbrella encompassing the pursuit of spectral entities (ghost hunting), the search for unknown animals (cryptozoology), the study of unidentified flying objects (ufology), and the practice of demonology—currently operates within a complete legal and ethical void. In stark contrast to professions that involve public trust and access to private spaces, such as licensed private investigators, uniformed security personnel, or certified psychological counselors, individuals and groups identifying as "paranormal investigators" are entirely unburdened by any requirement for professional licensure, mandatory criminal background checks, essential liability insurance, or adherence to any established, enforceable code of ethical standards.

This profound absence of governmental or self-regulatory oversight has inadvertently created a fertile and dangerous environment—a haven—for a wide spectrum of predatory and criminal behaviors. The consequences documented across numerous jurisdictions are alarming and include, but are not limited to:

- **Property-Related Crimes:** Unauthorized entry and **trespassing** onto private, commercial, and government-owned properties, often leading to property damage.

- **Financial and Consumer Fraud:** The perpetration of **fraud** through the sale of fraudulent services, misleading claims of spiritual cleansing, and the collection of fees for non-existent "evidence."
- **Psychological and Emotional Abuse:** The infliction of profound **psychological abuse** and trauma, particularly on vulnerable individuals seeking help, by fabricating evidence or misdiagnosing mental health issues as supernatural possession.
- **Sexual Violence:** A disturbing pattern of **sexual violence** and exploitation that capitalizes on the victims' emotional distress and the perceived "spiritual authority" of the investigators.
- **Negligent Death and Bodily Harm:** Acts of **negligent death** or serious injury resulting from investigators encouraging dangerous behavior, failing to report critical safety issues, or operating in hazardous locations without proper safety protocols.
- **Obstruction of Justice:** The **obstruction of justice** in legitimate criminal or missing persons cases by tampering with evidence, spreading false narratives, or unduly influencing witnesses and victims with paranormal explanations.

This detailed and critically supported report is therefore structured to articulate the urgent, overriding necessity for either the establishment of robust, legally-mandated **strict regulation**—mirroring that of legitimate investigative or therapeutic professions—or, failing the feasibility of effective control, an outright **ban** on the organized, commercial, and amateur pursuit of paranormal investigation groups. The imperative behind this action is the immediate and vital need to protect public safety and preserve legal integrity, with the argument anchored by the analysis of specific, documented case precedents and resulting criminal convictions.

2. Criminal Predation and Sexual Violence

The most critical and disturbing argument for the immediate professional regulation of the paranormal investigation field is the chilling effectiveness of the "paranormal investigator" or "ghost hunter" label as a sophisticated form of predatory camouflage. This guise provides a perfect, often socially accepted, means for sexual predators to access highly vulnerable victims and enter private homes or isolated locations without the scrutiny, background checks, or professional accountability that any legitimate service provider would face.

This is not a theoretical concern; it is a documented pattern with severe legal consequences:

Case Studies in Predatory Camouflage

- **The "Ghost Hunter" Rapist (David Lynn Turner):** This definitive case clearly illustrates the abuse of the paranormal label as a mechanism for isolation and assault. David Lynn Turner, ironically a former Texas reserve peace officer, weaponized the guise of a "paranormal investigator" to lure women into extremely vulnerable and remote settings. He meticulously cultivated a persona on social media, specifically targeting women who identified as "sensitive" or psychically attuned to spirits. By framing the encounters as necessary "investigations" at desolate, "haunted" locations, he was able to isolate his victims before sexually assaulting them. The legal system recognized the severity of this pre-meditated exploitation, and he was sentenced to 10 years in prison in 2022. This case is a stark warning that the lack of regulation allows a self-declared title to function as a tool for criminal enterprise.
- **The James Hydrick Precedent: The Narrative of "Special Gifts":** While often cited in the skeptical community as a prime example of psychic fraud—having been exposed by investigator

Dan Korem for faking his powers—James Hydrick's deeper criminal history reveals the lethal combination of claiming "special gifts" and predatory behavior. Hydrick was a convicted child molester who used his fraudulent claims of psychic power, combined with his role as a martial arts instructor, to groom and abuse children under his influence. The narrative of having a "special gift" is incredibly effective at creating a power dynamic that encourages victims, particularly children, to remain silent out of fear that their claims will be dismissed against the authority of the "gifted" individual. Tragically, in 2025, Hydrick was arrested again on serious charges related to Child Sexual Abuse Material (CSAM), underscoring how this exploitative narrative persists and continues to endanger vulnerable populations across decades.

- **Cult Dynamics and Spiritual Abuse (Terrill Dalton):** The intersection of spiritual or paranormal authority and sexual abuse creates an environment of total control, often mirroring the tactics of cults. Terrill Dalton, who operated in Idaho as a self-proclaimed "Holy Ghost" and cult leader, utilized a spiritual and paranormal lexicon to justify horrific crimes. He was convicted of raping both his own daughter and another woman, rationalizing these acts to his followers and victims as necessary "spiritual rituals" or "cleansings." This rationalization is alarmingly similar to the manipulative rhetoric used by unlicensed and unregulated demonologists or exorcists who claim to be performing a "spiritual procedure" on a victim, using the lack of oversight to bypass ethical and legal boundaries while perpetrating sexual assault.

The common thread across these cases is the unregulated "authority" granted by a self-declared paranormal title, which provides both access to victims and a powerful rhetorical shield to silence them. Regulation is therefore not merely a matter of consumer protection against fraud, but a critical imperative for public safety.

3. Domestic Violence and Negligent Homicide

The Dark Side of the Paranormal Pursuit: Toxicity, Negligence, and Fatal Outcomes

The contemporary subculture of "professional" ghost hunting, heavily influenced by media sensationalism, often fosters environments that are not just high-pressure and performative, but demonstrably toxic and dangerous, frequently leading to violence, injury, and death. The quest for paranormal proof, when unregulated and exploited for entertainment, carries profound and lethal risks for investigators, victims of associated crimes, and innocent property owners.The Human Cost of Media Stardom and Domestic Violence

The pressure to maintain a lucrative and compelling public persona as a "paranormal expert" can exacerbate underlying psychological issues and violent tendencies, with tragic consequences.

- **The Constantino Murder-Suicide:** The devastating case of Mark and Debby Constantino, key figures and featured experts on the popular Travel Channel series *Ghost Adventures*, serves as a stark reminder of the lethal intersection between fame and untreated domestic violence. Their public "investigator" personas and the associated media spotlight amplified the existing pressures in their turbulent relationship. In 2015, this escalating history of domestic violence reached a horrifying climax when Mark Constantino kidnapped Debby. The incident concluded with Mark murdering Debby and her male roommate in Sparks, Nevada, before ultimately taking his own life. This highly publicized tragedy did more than just expose the destructive nature of their relationship; it brought to light the critical lack of psychological screening, background checks, or any professional oversight for "experts" who are promoted and monetized by major media outlets and production companies. The industry's prioritization of compelling television over the mental well-being and public safety of its cast members was tragically illustrated.

Lethal Risks of Unregulated Urban Exploration

The pursuit of "haunted" or "spooky" locations often involves trespassing and illegal urban exploration, activities inherently fraught with physical danger and negligence, particularly in dilapidated or restricted areas.

- **The University of Toronto Fall:** The lure of an allegedly "haunted" location can override basic safety protocols, leading directly to fatal accidents. In a tragedy exemplifying this danger, a 29-year-old woman fell three stories to her death at 1 Spadina Crescent, a historical and structurally complex building on the University of Toronto campus, in 2009. The structure was well-known in local lore for being haunted. Police reports and subsequent investigation identified the activity preceding the fall as a "ghost hunt," during which the woman was exploring the building's roof, a high-risk area. This incident powerfully illustrates the lethal risks inherent in the unregulated, often late-night, and physically precarious activities associated with seeking out paranormal hotspots. The lack of proper safety equipment, training, and permission for entering such locations transforms a simple thrill-seeking activity into a matter of life and death [5].

Deadly Friction Between Trespassers and Property Owners

The culture of "ghost hunting" frequently involves illegal trespassing onto private property, which can lead to violent confrontations with homeowners defending their domicile against perceived criminal threats.

- **The "Spooky House" Shooting (Worthington, Ohio):** The distinction between "ghost hunter" and "trespasser" is often lost in the dark, leading to deadly misunderstandings. In 2006, a group of teenagers sought out a property in Worthington, Ohio, that was rumored to be haunted—a common destination for amateur thrill-seekers. While trespassing on the private property, the group was fired upon by the homeowner, Allen S. Davis. The confrontation resulted in one of the teenagers, Rachel Barezinsky, being permanently paralyzed. This incident starkly underscores the deadly friction and zero-tolerance response that can occur when amateur paranormal enthusiasts invade private space. For property owners, the trespass is often perceived not as a harmless ghost hunt, but as a potential home invasion or threat to safety, leading to lethal self-defense actions and permanent injury for those seeking a thrill [6].

---

4. Obstruction of Justice and Digital Vigilantism

The modern paranormal movement poses a significant and often underestimated systemic threat to the integrity of law enforcement operations, particularly through the phenomenon known as the "True Crime/Paranormal Crossover." The widespread adoption of social media platforms has allowed self-proclaimed psychics, amateur sleuths, and ghost hunters to inject themselves into active investigations, leading to tangible real-world consequences for police resources and the victims' families.

1. Direct Operational Interference: The Nicola Bulley Case

A stark illustration of this threat occurred during the 2023 search for missing mother Nicola Bulley in the United Kingdom.

- **Resource Diversion:** As the official police search by Lancashire Police was underway, the village became a focal point for what were termed "TikTok sleuths" and amateur ghost hunters. These individuals, driven by online notoriety and a belief in "spiritual" leads, descended upon the area.
- **Law Enforcement Response:** The influx of these civilian investigators, many of whom were streaming their activities live, became such a burden that Lancashire Police were compelled to issue **dispersal orders**. These orders were necessary to remove people who were actively disrupting the search.
- **Criminal and Disruptive Behavior:** The actions of these "investigators" went beyond mere curiosity. They were documented breaking into abandoned properties, harassing local residents for information or camera footage, and, most critically, forcing police to spend valuable time and manpower investigating **false "spiritual" leads** or responding to trespass and public order offenses, significantly distracting from the genuine search effort [7].

2. Legal Precedent and Defamation: The Idaho 4 Case

The intrusion of paranormal claims into criminal justice is not limited to physical interference; it now carries severe legal ramifications, as evidenced by the aftermath of the 2022 murders of four University of Idaho students.

- **Abuse of Platform:** Following the tragedy, TikTok personality Ashley Guillard utilized her platform and "spiritual tools"—specifically tarot cards—to conduct a public "reading" that falsely accused University of Idaho Professor Rebecca Scofield of orchestrating the brutal murders.

- **The Scofield v. Guillard Lawsuit:** Professor Scofield, whose reputation was instantly and widely damaged by the accusation, filed a defamation lawsuit against Guillard.
- **Establishment of Legal Limits:** A federal judge presiding over the case made a critical ruling, confirming that Guillard's "spiritual investigation" was indeed defamatory. The outcome of *Scofield v. Guillard* established a crucial legal precedent: claims of "paranormal intuition" or "psychic insight" cannot be used as an acceptable legal defense to shield an individual from liability for destroying a private citizen's reputation [8]. This ruling effectively drew a line, confirming that engaging in the True Crime/ Paranormal Crossover does not grant immunity from the laws of libel and slander.

---

5. Economic Vandalism and Fraud

The economic model underpinning many paranormal investigation groups is fundamentally exploitative and predatory, allowing them to accumulate content, views, and fame at the direct, long-term financial detriment of the property owners they purport to assist. This relationship is a critical ethical and legal failure within the unregulated pseudoscience community.The Financial Stigmatization of Property

The most significant financial threat posed by these investigations is the concept of a "stigmatized property," a phenomenon legally codified by amateur investigators themselves:

- **The *Stambovsky* Effect (Legal Haunting):** In the landmark 1991 case *Stambovsky v. Ackley*, the New York Supreme Court delivered a precedent-setting ruling. It determined that a property's former owner, by widely publicizing the home as haunted, had created a "condition" that materially impaired the value of the residence and was not easily discoverable by a buyer. The court ruled the house was, in effect, "legally haunted." This precedent means that when an amateur investigation group, seeking online fame, "confirms" a haunting on a client's property and publicizes their findings through social media, documentaries, or blogs, they are legally stigmatizing that property.

- **Mandatory Disclosure and Value Reduction:** This legally created stigma acts as a material defect. Sellers are often compelled by law to disclose the confirmed "haunting" to potential buyers, severely restricting the pool of interested parties and, more critically, significantly reducing the property's market value. The investigators profit from the views generated by the content, while the property owner incurs a long-term, uninsurable financial loss.

Deceptive Trade Practices and Consumer Fraud

Beyond the issue of property value, the operational methods of many paranormal groups constitute a form of consumer fraud, particularly when targeting vulnerable individuals:

- **Charging for Pseudo-Science Services:** Many investigation teams charge consultation fees, solicit substantial donations, or utilize paid subscription services (e.g., Patreon) to fund their "research." These services rely on the use of unvalidated equipment presented as scientific instruments.
- **The Gimmick of Randomization:** Devices such as "Spirit Boxes," "Ghost Meters," and Electronic Voice Phenomenon (EVP) recorders are the core tools of the trade. However, independent analysis demonstrates that devices like the Spirit Box function essentially as highly sensitive radio scanners or random word generators. Presenting the device's random output—be it white noise, fragmented radio signals, or contextually meaning-

less words—as evidence of intelligent communication with the deceased constitutes a deceptive trade practice.

- **Exploitation of the Vulnerable:** The primary clientele for these paid investigations are often grieving families, individuals struggling with mental health issues, or those experiencing genuine, but non-paranormal, home issues (e.g., structural noises, carbon monoxide poisoning). Investigators exploit the emotional vulnerability and desperate search for answers within these groups, offering a definitive, supernatural answer for a fee, all while ignoring credible, non-paranormal explanations. The lack of regulation allows these deceptive practices to continue unabated, effectively defrauding those most in need of genuine, compassionate assistance.

---

6. Conclusion and Legislative Recommendations

The unregulated field of "paranormal investigation" is an alarming societal vacuum—a phantom profession that exists entirely without formal definition, mandatory oversight, or fundamental accountability. This lack of structure has permitted a documented and disturbing pattern of criminal and unethical behavior, creating an irrefutable and urgent case for robust state and federal intervention. The documented association of individuals operating under this title with serious offenses, including sexual predation, malicious and unwarranted trespassing, acts rising to the level of negligent homicide, severe psychological abuse of vulnerable individuals, and deliberate obstruction of legitimate law enforcement and judicial processes, demonstrates a clear and present danger to public safety that can no longer be ignored.-----Proposed Regulatory Framework: An Act for Public Safety and Professional Accountability

A comprehensive legislative framework is essential to mitigate the public safety risks associated with this unregulated industry. The following statutes are proposed to bring this activity under the purview of established legal and professional standards.1. Mandatory Professional Licensing and Vetting

All individuals who market, charge a fee for, or present themselves to the public as "paranormal investigators," "ghost hunters," or similar titles must be legally required to hold a state-issued Private Investigator (PI) license. This requirement is non-negotiable and based on the fact that their activities—gathering information, surveillance, and entering private premises—mirror those of a licensed PI. Attaining this license would necessitate the following public safety safeguards:

- **Comprehensive Background Checks:** A mandatory, rigorous federal and state criminal background check.
- **Legal and Ethical Training:** Completion of a state-accredited course covering legal statutes, ethical conduct, privacy laws, and the limitations of their authority.
- **Fingerprinting and Registration:** Submission of biometric data for full registration with the relevant state licensing board, ensuring their identity and operational location are known to the authorities.
- **Liability Insurance:** Proof of professional liability insurance to protect the public from financial damages resulting from negligence or misconduct.

2. "Bounty Hunter" Classification and Operational Constraints

Due to the inherently high-risk, high-stress, and quasi-law-enforcement nature of many "paranormal investigations"—which often involve operating under cover of darkness, entering emotionally charged situations, and dealing with potentially volatile individuals—investigators must be classified under strict statutes similar to those governing Bail Enforcement Agents (Bounty Hunters). This classification would impose:

- **Weapon Restrictions:** Prohibitions on carrying firearms or other lethal weapons while on "investigation" unless they possess a separate, valid, and required armed PI license.
- **Mandatory Use-of-Force Training:** Required training, even if unarmed, on de-escalation tactics and legal constraints on physical interaction with the public.
- **Chain of Custody Protocols:** Standardized procedures for documenting, preserving, and reporting any evidence or findings, particularly if they suspect an actual crime has occurred, to prevent the contamination of potential crime scenes or legal proceedings.

3. The "Medical Clearance" Act: Protection Against Exploitation and Abuse

To prevent the dangerous and abusive practice of non-medical personnel intervening in cases of suspected mental illness, it must be made a felony to perform or recommend an exorcism, "spiritual cleansing," or any similar non-medical intervention on a person believed to be afflicted by a paranormal entity **without prior, signed clearance from a licensed psychiatrist or clinical psychologist.** This Act serves to:

- **Rule Out Mental Illness:** Ensure that individuals experiencing hallucinations, delusions, or other symptoms are first medically evaluated and offered appropriate mental healthcare.
- **Prevent Psychological Harm:** Criminalize the act of profiting from or inflicting further psychological trauma on individuals whose distress is rooted in a treatable medical condition.

- **Mandatory Reporting:** Require any individual who suspects mental illness during an investigation to immediately cease their activities and refer the client to a medical professional.

4. Criminalize "Haunted" Trespass and Property Vandalism

The penalties for trespassing must be significantly enhanced when the offense is committed for the express purpose of "paranormal research," "ghost hunting," or similar activities. This specific enhancement aims to deter amateur and reckless groups who routinely invade private and secured property, often causing property damage and intimidating residents.

- **Felony Enhancement:** Trespassing on secured or clearly posted private property with the intent of conducting a "paranormal investigation" must be classified as an aggravated felony, carrying greater fines and potential prison time than simple trespass.
- **Restitution Mandate:** Any conviction must include a mandatory order for full financial restitution to the property owner for all damages and security costs incurred.
- **Loss of License:** For licensed investigators, a conviction under this enhanced statute must result in the immediate and permanent revocation of their Private Investigator license.

---

7. References

1. **State of Texas v. David Lynn Turner.** (2022). *San Jacinto County District Court.* (Sentenced to 10 years for sexual assault under the guise of ghost hunting).
2. **State of South Carolina v. James Allen Hydrick.** (2025). *Lexington County Sheriff's Department.* (Arrested for Child Sex-

ual Abuse Material; previously convicted of child molestation in 1989).

3. **State of Idaho v. Terrill Dalton.** (2021). (Cult leader convicted of rape; operated under spiritual/paranormal pretenses).
4. **Reno Police Department Report.** (2015, September). *Investigation into the deaths of Mark and Debby Constantino.*
5. **Toronto Police Service Report.** (2009, September). *Fatal Fall at 1 Spadina Crescent.* (Reported in *The Toronto Star*, "Ghost hunt on Gothic rooftop turns tragic").
6. **State of Ohio v. Allen S. Davis.** (2007). *Franklin County Common Pleas Court.* (Convicted of felonious assault regarding the shooting of Rachel Barezinsky).
7. **Lancashire Constabulary Press Conference.** (2023, February 15). *Statement regarding public interference in the Nicola Bulley investigation.*
8. **Scofield v. Guillard.** (2024). *United States District Court for the District of Idaho.* (Summary judgment ruling that tarot readings are not a defense against defamation).
9. **Stambovsky v. Ackley.** (1991). 169 A.D.2d 254 (N.Y. App. Div.). (The "Ghostbusters Ruling" regarding stigmatized property).

LEGAL NOTICE & CEASE AND DESIST TEMPLATES

Disclaimer: *The following documents are templates for educational and drafting purposes only. They do not constitute legal advice. Laws regarding trespass, defamation, and property liability vary significantly by jurisdiction (State/Country). You should consult with a qualified attorney to customize these statutes to your specific local codes.*

DOCUMENT A: NOTICE AGAINST TRESPASS & DEMAND FOR PRESERVATION OF PROPERTY VALUE

Target Audience: Private Property Owners, Business Owners, or Historical Societies. **Purpose:** To formally bar paranormal groups from a property and establish liability for "stigmatized property" damages if they publish claims about the location.

[YOUR NAME/BUSINESS NAME] [Street Address] [City, State, Zip Code]

[DATE]

VIA CERTIFIED MAIL R.R.R. To: [Name of Paranormal Group / Individual Leader] [Address / Social Media Handle / Email]

RE: FORMAL NOTICE OF NO TRESPASS AND CEASE AND DESIST

Dear [Name of Group/Individual]:

This letter serves as formal legal notice that you, your agents, affiliates, and any associated "investigation teams" are **strictly prohibited** from entering, remaining upon, or surveilling the property located at: **[Insert Address of Property]**.

1. CRIMINAL TRESPASS NOTICE Pursuant to **[Insert Local Penal Code, e.g., California Penal Code § 602 / Texas Penal Code § 30.05]**, any entry onto this property is unauthorized. We have a zero-tolerance policy. Be advised that in *State of Ohio v. Allen S. Davis* (2007), the courts recognized the extreme dangers inherent in unauthorized "ghost hunting" trespass. To ensure the physical safety of all parties, local law enforcement has been notified to arrest any unauthorized persons found on the premises.

2. LIABILITY FOR "STIGMATIZED PROPERTY" DAMAGES Be advised that your activities—specifically the publication of videos, audio, or articles claiming this property is "haunted," "demonic," or otherwise paranormally active—constitute a direct threat to the financial value of this asset.

Under the legal doctrine established in ** *Stambovsky v. Ackley* (169 A.D.2d 254) **, publicizing a property as haunted can legally classify it as "stigmatized," significantly reducing its market value and creating burdensome disclosure requirements for the owner.

- **Warning:** If you publish any content alleging paranormal activity at this location, we will hold you **civilly liable** for any diminution in the property's market value, which may amount to **[Insert Estimated Property Value Drop, e.g., $50,000+]**. We will seek actual damages, punitive damages, and legal fees for the creation of this stigma.

3. DEFAMATION AND PRIVACY (THE "SCOFIELD" NOTICE) We are aware of the trend to "psychically investigate" private citizens. Pursuant to the federal ruling in ** *Scofield v. Guillard* (2024) **, claims made by "psychics" or "intuitives" are **not protected opinion** if they falsely accuse residents of crimes or moral turpitude. Any public statement implying that the owners are involved in nefarious, cult-like, or criminal activity based on "spiritual evidence" will result in immediate defamation litigation.

4. DEMAND TO CEASE You are hereby demanded to:

1. Cease all physical attempts to access the property.
2. Cease all digital surveillance or drone overflights.
3. Refrain from publishing any "investigations" regarding this specific address.

GOVERN YOURSELF ACCORDINGLY.

Sincerely,
[Signature]
[Printed Name] [Title, if applicable]

DOCUMENT B: LAW ENFORCEMENT ADVISORY LETTER

Target Audience: Police Departments or City Councils issuing warnings to known "UrbEx" or Paranormal groups operating in their jurisdiction. **Purpose:** To warn groups that "investigation" is not a valid defense for criminal activity and obstruction.

[CITY/COUNTY] POLICE DEPARTMENT [Department Header/Seal]

[DATE]

RE: ADVISORY REGARDING INTERFERENCE AND TRESPASS ("PARANORMAL INVESTIGATION")

To Whom It May Concern:

The **[City/County]** Police Department is issuing this advisory regarding the rise of amateur "paranormal investigation" and "urban exploration" groups within our jurisdiction. While we respect the right to free assembly, "ghost hunting" does not grant immunity from state and local laws.

NOTICE OF ENFORCEMENT PROTOCOLS:

1. ZERO TOLERANCE FOR "HAUNTED" TRESPASS Individuals found entering abandoned, public, or private structures under the guise of "research" will be charged with **Criminal Trespass** under **[Insert State Code]**.

- **Safety Hazard:** Officers are aware of the *University of Toronto (2009)* precedent involving fatalities during such activities. For officer and public safety, all unauthorized presence in secured structures will be treated as a potential felony burglary in progress until proven otherwise.

2. OBSTRUCTION OF JUSTICE (THE "NICOLA BULLEY" PRECEDENT) Be advised that interfering with active crime scenes, missing persons searches, or police perimeters to "communicate with spirits" is a criminal offense.

- Following the *Lancashire Constabulary (2023)* findings regarding the Nicola Bulley investigation, this Department will charge any individual who breaches a police cordon or harasses victims' families with **Obstruction of Justice** and **Disorderly Conduct**. "Psychic tips" or "visions" do not authorize you to enter restricted areas or contact witnesses.

3. POSSESSION OF BURGLARY TOOLS The possession of crowbars, lockpicks, or bolt cutters—often carried by groups to access "haunted" sites—will be prosecuted as **Possession of Criminal Tools**, regardless of the intent to "just look around."

4. FALSE REPORTING Calling emergency services to report "demonic activity" or requesting welfare checks on "cursed" individuals diverts critical resources. Such actions will be prosecuted as **Misuse of 911/False Reporting**.

This Department urges all amateur groups to cease unregulated operations immediately.

[Name] [Rank/Title] [Department Name]

PROPERTY STIGMA PREVENTION & DEFENSE CHECKLIST

Purpose: To establish a documented history of "Quiet Enjoyment" and prevent your property from being legally or socially classified as "stigmatized" (haunted/psychologically impacted) by third parties.

Principle: In *Stambovsky v. Ackley*, the court ruled a house was haunted as a matter of law largely because the *owner* had promoted it as such. This checklist does the opposite: it creates an evidentiary trail that the property is normal, peaceful, and quiet, countering any "investigator" claims.

PHASE 1: DOCUMENTATION OF QUIET ENJOYMENT

The goal here is to prove that the "haunting" is an external fabrication, not an internal reality.

- **[ ] Establish a "Quiet Enjoyment" Log:**
    - Create a simple physical or digital logbook.

  - **Action:** Once a month, record a simple entry: *"Property is quiet. No unusual noises, disturbances, or third-party interference observed."*
  - **Why:** If a paranormal group claims your house was "active" on a specific date, you have a contemporaneous record stating otherwise.
- [ ] **Environmental Baseline Testing:**
  - **Action:** If rumors persist, hire a licensed home inspector to test for:
    - **Carbon Monoxide (CO):** Levels should be zero.
    - **Infrasound/Vibrations:** Check for loose HVAC units or nearby industrial hums.
    - **Drafts/Thermal Leaks:** Identify "cold spots" as insulation failures.
  - **Why:** You are converting "paranormal evidence" into "deferred maintenance." If someone claims a "demon" is in the basement, you can produce a report showing it's actually an unsealed window or a high EMF reading from an old fuse box.
- [ ] **The "Non-Disclosure" Policy:**
  - **Action:** Strictly forbid family members or tenants from joking about ghosts on social media or in local interviews.
  - **Why:** Your own words are the strongest evidence against you in a *Stambovsky* situation. Denial must be consistent.

PHASE 2: PHYSICAL HARDENING (ACCESS DENIAL)

Paranormal claims often rely on "urban legends" fueled by easy access to the property.

- [ ] **Explicit Signage (Photography Ban):**
    - **Action:** Post "No Trespassing" signs that explicitly include: *"Private Property. No Photography or Video Recording for Commercial Purposes Without Written Consent."*
    - **Why:** While you can't always stop people from filming from a public sidewalk, posting this at the boundary creates a basis for a "theft of services" or "commercial appropriation" argument if they monetize the footage.
- [ ] **Motion-Activated Lighting & Audio:**
    - **Action:** Install bright, motion-sensor floodlights.
    - **Why:** "Ghost hunters" rely on darkness and "spooky" atmosphere. Blasting the area with 5000 lumens of LED light ruins their video aesthetic and makes the location look clinical rather than haunted.
- [ ] **Perimeter Cameras (The "Anti-Orb" Evidence):**
    - **Action:** Install high-definition cameras (4K preferred) covering the yard/entry points.
    - **Why:** If a group claims they saw a "shadow figure" on your lawn at 2 AM, your crystal-clear footage of a stray cat or a tree branch effectively debunks them, protecting your property value.

PHASE 3: DIGITAL DEFENSE & MONITORING

Stop the "legend" before it goes viral.

- [ ] **Set Google Alerts:**
  - **Action:** Set up daily alerts for your specific address and street name.
  - **Why:** Catch mentions of your home on Reddit (r/Paranormal), YouTube, or TikTok immediately.
- [ ] **DMCA Takedown Strategy:**
  - **Action:** If a video is posted that was filmed *on* your property (trespassing), file a DMCA (Digital Millennium Copyright Act) takedown notice with YouTube/TikTok immediately, citing privacy violation and unauthorized commercial use of private property.
  - **Why:** De-platforming the content removes the incentive for copycats.
- [ ] **Pre-Drafted "Cease and Desist" (See Document A):**
  - **Action:** Have the template from our previous session ready. Send it immediately to any channel or "investigator" that features your home.

PHASE 4: SELLER DISCLOSURE STRATEGY (IF SELLING)

How to sell a house rumors say is haunted without losing value.

- [ ] **The "Material Defect" Statement:**

  - **Action:** In your seller disclosures, you can preemptively state: *"Seller has no knowledge of any paranormal activity, hauntings, or stigmatizing events associated with the property. Any third-party claims regarding such are expressly denied and unsubstantiated."*
  - **Why:** This shifts the burden of proof. You are legally going on record that the house is normal.
- [ ] **Warranty of Quiet Possession:**
  - **Action:** Offer a standard warranty deed that guarantees "quiet possession."
  - **Why:** It reinforces that the property is legally sound and free of "encumbrances" (which, in a legal sense, includes squatters or nuisance claims).

DIGITAL HARASSMENT...

DIGITAL HARASSMENT & CYBERSTALKING EVIDENCE CHECKLIST

Purpose: To guide victims of paranormal-related digital harassment (doxxing, threats, swatting, relentless messaging) in gathering admissible evidence for a police report. **Disclaimer:** *Police departments often dismiss online harassment as "civil disputes." This checklist is designed to translate your experience into the language of criminal law: "Pattern of Conduct," "Credible Threat," and "Intimidation."*

PHASE 1: PRESERVATION (DO NOT DELETE ANYTHING)

The golden rule of digital forensics: Never delete the evidence, even if it is distressing. If the harasser deletes their posts, you must have a copy.

- [ ] **The "Rule of Three" Screenshots:**
    - For every harassing post/message, take three distinct screenshots:

1. **The Content:** The message/post itself.
2. **The Context:** The entire thread/conversation showing you did not provoke it.
3. **The Profile:** The harasser's profile page (URL, bio, follower count) at that moment.

- [ ] **URL Preservation (Wayback Machine):**
  - **Action:** Copy the specific URL of the harassing tweet, video, or post. Paste it into the **Internet Archive (Wayback Machine)** or **archive.today**.
  - **Why:** Screenshots can be faked (Photoshop). An archived link is a third-party, timestamped verification that the content existed.
- [ ] **Email Header Extraction:**
  - **Action:** If harassed via email, do *not* just print the body text. You need the "Full Headers" (Metadata).
  - **Why:** Headers contain the sender's originating IP address, which police can use to geotag the suspect even if they use a fake name.
- [ ] **Native File Export:**
  - **Action:** If they send voicemails or videos, download the actual file (MP3/MP4) to a USB drive. Do not rely on the app (e.g., Messenger) keeping it hosted.

PHASE 2: ESTABLISHING "PATTERN OF CONDUCT"

Criminal stalking requires a "course of conduct"—two or more acts showing a continuity of purpose.

- [ ] **The Chronological Incident Log (Excel/Notebook):**
  - Create a spreadsheet with the following columns:
    - **Date/Time:** (e.g., "Feb 7, 2026, 10:45 PM")
    - **Platform:** (e.g., "TikTok Comment")
    - **User Handle:** (e.g., "@GhostHunterX_99")
    - **Nature of Act:** (e.g., "Threat to burn down house," "Posted my home address")
    - **Witnesses:** (Did anyone else see it/like it?)
    - **Impact:** (e.g., "Caused panic attack," "Forced me to lock business")
- [ ] **Cross-Platform Linking:**
  - **Action:** Document if the same user is following you across different apps (e.g., banned on Facebook -> appears on Instagram).
  - **Why:** This proves "willful and malicious intent" to bypass your boundaries, a key element of stalking statutes.

PHASE 3: DOCUMENTING "DOXXING" & REAL-WORLD THREATS

This is where "trolling" crosses into "Danger to Life/Property."

- [ ] **Search Your Own Address:**
  - **Action:** Check if they have posted your address, phone number, or workplace.
  - **Evidence:** Screenshot the post *and* the comments. (e.g., Followers saying "Let's pay them a visit.")

    - **Why:** This is evidence of "Incitement to Violence" or "Terroristic Threats."
- [ ] **The "Swatting" Pre-Check:**
    - **Action:** If they threaten to call police on you ("Swatting"), screenshot that specific threat immediately.
    - **Why:** If police *do* show up at your door, showing them this screenshot immediately can de-escalate the situation and turn the investigation back onto the caller.

PHASE 4: DEMONSTRATING "SUBSTANTIAL DISTRESS"

To upgrade harassment to a felony in many jurisdictions, you must prove it caused you significant suffering.

- [ ] **Financial Impact Log:**
    - Did you buy security cameras? New locks?
    - Did you miss work due to stress?
    - Did you pay a lawyer or IT expert?
    - **Action:** Keep *all* receipts. This moves the crime from "annoyance" to "economic injury."
- [ ] **Medical/Psychological Records:**
    - **Action:** If you visited a doctor or therapist for anxiety/insomnia related to the harassment, request a simple note confirming the visit date and cause.

PHASE 5: FILING THE REPORT (SCRIPT)

When you go to the station, use this script to ensure they take a report rather than turning you away.

Do NOT say: *"Someone is being mean to me online."* (They will say: "Block them.") **DO say:** *"I am here to report a criminal* ***Course of Conduct*** *involving* ***Cyberstalking*** *and* ***Credible Threats of Violence.****"*

The Script:

"Officer, I am the victim of a targeted harassment campaign by [Suspect Name/Handle].

1. They have contacted me **[Number]** times despite being told to stop (Criminal Trespass/Harassment).
2. They have posted my private address to incite others (Doxxing/Endangerment).
3. I have a **preservation log** of [Number] incidents proving a 'continuity of purpose.'
4. I am fearful for my safety and am requesting a **report number** for my records to seek a Protective Order."

PLATFORM TAKEDOWN...

PLATFORM TAKEDOWN & DATA PRESERVATION REQUEST TEMPLATES

Disclaimer: *These templates are designed to escalate a report beyond the standard "Flag" button. They are written for the "Legal" or "Trust & Safety" departments of major platforms (YouTube, TikTok, Meta, X). While powerful, they do not guarantee removal unless a clear Terms of Service (ToS) violation or legal infringement has occurred.*

CONCEPTUAL OVERVIEW: WHICH TEMPLATE TO USE?

Before sending, you must choose the correct legal argument. Using the wrong one (e.g., filing a DMCA for a video you didn't film) can get your request rejected or even get your account banned for perjury.

- **Use TEMPLATE A (Privacy/Harassment)** if: They filmed you without consent, posted your address (doxxing), or are encouraging followers to attack you.
- **Use TEMPLATE B (DMCA Copyright)** if: They used *your* photo, *your* video, or *your* artwork in their content without permission.

TEMPLATE A: FORMAL TAKEDOWN & PRESERVATION REQUEST (Harassment/Privacy)

Target: Legal Department / Trust & Safety Team

Subject: URGENT: Legal Takedown Request - Severe Harassment, Doxxing, and Privacy Violation

[DATE]

VIA EMAIL / LEGAL WEBFORM

To: Legal Department, **[Platform Name, e.g., YouTube / TikTok]**

From: [Your Full Legal Name]

Re: https://dictionary.cambridge.org/us/dictionary/english/offending

To the Trust & Safety Team:

I am writing to formally report a severe violation of your Terms of Service and Community Guidelines regarding **Harassment, Doxxing, and Invasion of Privacy**. The content hosted on your platform is currently being used to incite targeted harassment against me and threatens my physical safety.

1. IDENTIFICATION OF INFRINGING CONTENT

- **Channel/User Name: [Name of Harasser]**
- **Video/Post Title: [Title]**
- **URL: [Insert Direct Link]**
- **Timestamp (if video): [e.g., 02:14 - 02:45]**

2. SPECIFIC VIOLATIONS OF [PLATFORM NAME] GUIDELINES

This content violates your specific policies on:

- **Doxxing/PII:** The user reveals my **[Home Address / Phone Number / Workplace]** without my consent. This puts me at risk of "swatting" and physical harm.
- **Targeted Harassment:** The user explicitly calls for their followers to **[harass/contact/visit]** me. This constitutes a "Call to Action" for brigading.
- **Privacy:** The video was filmed on private property **[Address]** where the user was trespassing. I have a reasonable expectation of privacy in my own home.

3. LEGAL NOTICE & DEMAND FOR REMOVAL

Under the laws of **[Your State/Country]**, this conduct constitutes **[Cyberstalking / Criminal Harassment / Invasion of Privacy]**. I have filed a preliminary report with **[Name of Police Dept]** (Report #**[Insert Number if available]**).

I demand the **IMMEDIATE REMOVAL** of the content listed above to mitigate further damages.

4. PRESERVATION OF EVIDENCE (SPOLIATION NOTICE)

DO NOT DELETE THE USER DATA ASSOCIATED WITH THIS ACCOUNT.

Pursuant to *18 U.S.C. § 2703(f)* (or equivalent local statute), I request that you **preserve all records** associated with this account—including IP logs, login history, and direct messages—pending the issuance of a subpoena or court order. If this evidence is deleted after this notice, we will treat it as **Spoliation of Evidence**.

I declare under penalty of perjury that the information in this notice is accurate and that I am the victim of the conduct described above.

Sincerely,
[Your Signature]
[Your Printed Name]
[Your Phone Number]

TEMPLATE B: DMCA COPYRIGHT TAKEDOWN NOTICE

Target: Copyright Agent

Subject: DMCA Takedown Notice - Unauthorized Use of Copyrighted Material

[DATE]

To: Copyright Agent, **[Platform Name]**

1. The Copyright Owner:

I, **[Your Name]**, am the sole copyright owner of the material described below.

2. The Infringed Work:

The copyrighted work is **[Describe your original photo/video, e.g., "A photograph of my living room taken by me on Jan 1, 2024"]**.

- *Optional:* Link to where you originally posted it: **https://www.facebook.com/help/424946150928896**

3. The Infringing Material:

The infringing copy is located at: **https://www.youtube.com/playlist?list=PLh6tmn_6jFF5EYwRmSMServK3JolKvHiV**.

The infringement occurs at timestamp: **[e.g., 00:15 - 00:30]**.

4. Statement of Good Faith:

I have a good faith belief that the use of the material in the manner complained of is not authorized by the copyright owner, its agent, or the law.

5. Statement of Accuracy:

The information in this notification is accurate, and under penalty of perjury, I am the owner of an exclusive right that is allegedly infringed.

[Your Signature]

[Your Address, Phone Number, Email]

QUICK-FIND GUIDE: WHERE TO SEND THESE

Don't just use the "Report" button. Use the dedicated legal forms/ emails for a paper trail.

Platform	Contact Method	Best For...
YouTube	copyright@youtube.com OR Legal Removal Webform	Privacy complain Copyright.
TikTok	legal@tiktok.com OR Privacy Report Form	Doxxing & "Hat
Meta (FB/ Insta)	Help Center > Legal Rights	IP infringement. in-app "Report" but
X (Twitter)	Help Center > Report a Violation	Doxxing (Private
Cloudflare	abuse@cloudflare.com	If they have a *pri* Cloudflare shielding

THE DIGITAL DECEPTION CHECKLIST

Why Vigilance Against Digital Manipulation Matters

In the past, a "ghost photo" was likely a double exposure or a speck of dust on a lens—a curiosity, but rarely a crime. Today, the landscape has shifted dangerously. With the rise of **Deepfakes** (AI-generated video/ audio) and **Generative AI**, bad actors can now manufacture "evidence" that is virtually indistinguishable from reality to the naked eye.

Watching for these signs is not just about skepticism; it is a matter of **financial and emotional self-defense**.

1. **Prevention of Emotional Fraud:** Predators now use AI voice cloning to mimic deceased loved ones, manipulating grieving families into believing they are communicating with the dead. This is a form of psychological abuse used to extract money for "mediumship" services.
2. **Protection Against Property Stigma:** Unscrupulous creators can digitally insert "demons" into footage of your home or business to generate viral content. Once millions of viewers believe your property is "infested," the real-world value of your asset drops, and your privacy is destroyed.

3. **Legal Accountability:** In a court of law, "digital evidence" is increasingly scrutinized. By understanding how to spot a fake, you protect yourself from being liable for—or a victim of—fraudulent claims that waste police resources and clog the justice system.

In the digital age, seeing is no longer believing. Verification is the only truth.

Forensic Analysis of Paranormal Evidence & AI Fabrication

Purpose: To empower property owners, victims, and skeptics to identify manufactured "evidence." **Context:** The modern paranormal industry is currently flooded with "Generative AI" and "Deepfake" technology. An investigator may present you with a photo of a "demon" in your hallway or an audio recording of your deceased relative. In many cases, these are not spiritual manifestations; they are digital renderings created in seconds using commercially available software.

Use this checklist to audit any "evidence" presented to you.

---

1. VISUAL FORENSICS: DETECTING AI & DEEPFAKES

Generative AI tools (like Midjourney, DALL-E, or Photoshop's Generative Fill) can insert "ghosts" into photos that look terrifyingly real at first glance. Here is how to spot the flaws.

- [ ] **The "Glossy" Texture Check:**
    - **Look for:** A hyper-smooth, painterly, or plastic-like texture on the "entity."
    - **The Flaw:** AI struggles with the "grain" (noise) of a real low-light photograph. If the room is grainy and dark, but the ghost is sharp and smooth, it is a digital insertion.
- [ ] **Shadow & Lighting Mismatch:**

    - **Look for:** Shadows cast by the "entity" that do not match the light sources in the room.
    - **The Flaw:** If the light is coming from a window on the left, but the ghost has a shadow on the left, it was pasted in.
- [ ] **Anatomy Hallucinations:**
    - **Look for:** Too many fingers, merging limbs, or nonsensical clothing (e.g., a shirt blending into a wall).
    - **The Flaw:** Generative AI notoriously struggles with hands and defined edges. A "demonic claw" with six fingers is likely a render error, not a mutation.
- [ ] **The "Stock Asset" Trap:**
    - **Action:** Take the "ghost photo" and run it through **Google Lens** or **TinEye** (Reverse Image Search).
    - **The Reality:** Many investigators use "Ghost in Photo" mobile apps that paste the same pre-made "spooky girl" or "shadow man" png files into images.

---

2. AUDIO FORENSICS: EVPs & AI VOICE CLONING

Investigators often claim to capture "Electronic Voice Phenomena" (EVP). Modern tech allows them to clone voices or synthesize speech to say exactly what you want to hear.

- [ ] **The "Too Clean" Frequency:**
    - **Look for:** A voice that has zero background hiss, static, or room tone, sounding like it was recorded in a studio.
    - **The Flaw:** Real field recordings are dirty. If the "ghost voice" sounds like a crisp podcast host while the investigator sounds muffled, it is a text-to-speech overlay.
- [ ] **The "Spirit Box" Radio Sweep:**

- **Look for:** Full sentences coming through a sweeping radio device.
- **The Reality:** A Spirit Box sweeps radio stations. It *should* only catch snippets ("...weather..." "...car sale..."). If it speaks a full, grammatical sentence ("*Get out of this house now*"), it is statistically impossible for that to be radio fragments. It is likely a pre-loaded audio file or a rigged device (e.g., the DR60 recorder loop).

- [ ] **Emotional Flatness (AI Cloning):**
  - **Look for:** A voice that sounds like your deceased loved one but lacks the correct inflection or emotional weight.
  - **The Flaw:** AI can clone the *timbre* of a voice from a 3-second sample (which they can get from your social media), but it struggles with human *cadence*. It often sounds "robotic" or monotone.

---

3. TEXTUAL & HISTORICAL FABRICATION

Some investigators will claim to have "researched the history" of your property to find tragedies that justify a haunting. They often use ChatGPT to invent this history.

- [ ] **The "Primary Source" Demand:**
  - **Action:** If they claim, *"A murderer named Silas Graves died here in 1892,"* demand to see the **Census Record**, **Death Certificate**, or **Newspaper scan**.
  - **The Check:** Do not accept a typed report or a screenshot of a text block. If they cannot produce the primary document, the person likely does not exist.
- [ ] **Hallucinated Geography:**
  - **Look for:** Mentions of street names, asylums, or businesses that never existed in your town.

  - **The Flaw:** Large Language Models (LLMs) like ChatGPT are "prediction engines," not search engines. They will confidently invent a "St. Mary's Orphanage" in your town to fit a spooky narrative because it sounds plausible.
- [ ] **The "Vague Tragedy" Trope:**
  - **Look for:** Generic stories that lack specifics (e.g., "A little girl fell down a well," "A witch lived in the woods").
  - **The Reality:** Real history is specific. Fake history is generic.

---

4. EQUIPMENT & APP MANIPULATION

The tools themselves are often designed to deceive.

- [ ] **The SLS Camera (Stick Figures):**
  - **The Tech:** This uses the Xbox Kinect sensor to map skeletons onto people for video games.
  - **The Flaw:** The sensor is aggressive; it tries to find skeletons in *anything*. If it maps a stick figure onto a coat rack or a chair, investigators call it a "demon sitting down." It is actually just a software glitch called **Pareidolia**.
- [ ] **"Ghost Radar" Mobile Apps:**
  - **The Tech:** Phones do not have "ghost sensors." They have magnetometers (compasses) and accelerometers.
  - **The Flaw:** Most ghost apps are programmed **Random Number Generators (RNG)**. They are toys designed to spit out "scary words" (Death, Kill, Run) at random intervals to entertain the user. They are not measuring anything in your environment.
- [ ] **The "Flashlight Trick":**

- **The Claim:** A flashlight turns on and off to answer "Yes/No" questions.
- **The Reality:** This is simple physics. As the bulb heats up, the connection expands and breaks (off). As it cools, it reconnects (on). It is a thermal cycle, not a spirit. *Always demand they use a click-on/click-off flashlight, not a twist-top Maglite.*

---

5. METADATA AUDIT (THE SMOKING GUN)

If you are given a digital file as "proof," check the digital fingerprint.

- [ ] **EXIF Data Inspection:**
    - **Action:** Right-click the photo file -> Properties -> Details (Windows) or "Get Info" (Mac).
    - **Look for:** Under "Program Name" or "Software," does it say **Adobe Photoshop**, **FaceApp**, or **Midjourney**?
    - **The Reality:** An original photo should say the camera model (e.g., "iPhone 13 Pro" or "Canon DSLR"). If the metadata has been scrubbed (blank) or lists editing software, the image has been manipulated.

CONCLUSION

THE EXORCISM OF INDIFFERENCE

Reclaiming Our Safety from the Shadows

We began this book with a simple premise: that the "paranormal" is not a lawless frontier, but a human industry subject to human laws. Over the course of these chapters, we have peeled back the layers of a multi-million dollar economy that trades in fear, grief, and curiosity. We have seen how the lack of regulation has transformed "ghost hunting" from a harmless hobby into a vector for stalking, fraud, and sexual predation.

The stories we have documented—of David Lynn Turner's calculated assaults, of the Constantino tragedy, of the homeowners held hostage by viral "haunting" hoaxes—are not isolated anomalies. They are the inevitable symptoms of a system that demands no accountability.

The Real "Poltergeist" is Human Behavior

Throughout this text, we have avoided debating the theological or scientific validity of the supernatural. That was intentional. The danger discussed in these pages does not come from the dead; it comes from the living.

- It is not a ghost that breaks into your home at 3:00 AM to film a TikTok video; it is a **trespasser**.
- It is not a demon that convinces a grieving mother to pay $5,000 to speak to her lost child; it is a **con artist**.
- It is not a spirit that grooms a child by telling them they are a "chosen vessel"; it is a **predator**.

When we strip away the spooky music and the night-vision filters, we are left with standard criminal behaviors that have simply found a clever disguise. The "paranormal" label functions as a "Get Out of Jail Free" card, allowing actions that would be arrested in any other context to be dismissed as "eccentric research."

The Cost of Silence (Ostension)

Sociologists use a term called **"Ostension"**—the process by which people act out legends, turning a story into reality. When a community tolerates the myth that a local house is "demonic," they are participating in ostension. They are implicitly inviting the vandals, the arsonists, and the harassers to descend upon that property. By remaining silent, by treating these groups as harmless entertainment, we are complicit in the "legend tripping" that destroys neighborhoods and lives. The cost of this indifference is paid by the family who cannot sell their stigmatized home, by the business owner harassed by "investigators," and by the vulnerable individuals who turn to charlatans instead of doctors for their mental health.

Your Final Charge

You now hold the toolkit necessary to fight back.

- **To the Legislator:** You have the framework to draft bills that require licensing, background checks, and insurance for this industry. The precedent exists; it simply needs to be applied.

- **To the Law Enforcement Officer:** You have the statutes to prosecute "haunted" trespass and digital stalking not as civil grievances, but as criminal acts.
- **To the Citizen:** You have the checklists to verify evidence, the templates to demand privacy, and the knowledge to spot a predator hiding behind a pendulum.

Closing the Gate

We often hear that "evil" needs an invitation to enter. For too long, our society has left the door wide open for the paranormal industry, rolling out a red carpet for those who would exploit our deepest fears.

This book is your instruction manual for closing that door. It is time to stop fearing the dark and start regulating the people hiding within it. The ghosts can do what they want—but the *ghost hunters* must answer to us.

www.ingramcontent.com/pod-product-compliance
Lightning Source LLC
LaVergne TN
LVHW022030200926
848481LV00007B/2623
* 9 7 9 8 3 4 8 5 1 0 5 7 2 *